Into the Beautiful

Mystery

Poetry by Montana Artists

S. E. Thomas, M.A., Editor

Into the Beautiful
Mystery
Poetry by Montana Artists
Volume V

S. E. Thomas, M.A., Editor

Published by The Dramatic Pen Press, L.L.C.

Lolo, Montana

Cover Image Taken by S. E. Thomas
in the Lewis & Clark Caverns
Whitehall, Montana

A great many thanks to the hardworking

English and literature teachers across our beautiful state.

May your legacy of beauty continue to flourish

long after we are gone.

Table of Contents

Poems by Adults

The Secret in the Bookshelf

A hidden story lurks nearby,
But does not have a name;
A mystery can be discovered,
There is no one to blame.

Unless you discover the secret of the shelf,
The past will stay the same,
And everything that was discovered,
Will never have its fame.

A secret love tells a tale,
But leaves the pages blank;
And everyone will wonder why,
A writer seeks to create.

Unless a writer has a story,
And writes both day and night;
The bookshelf will stay empty,
The secret is to write!

So write about your passion,
Don't let them slip by,
Write for all to hear your story,
And the bookshelf can keep its secret.

Rakayle Hier

About the Author

Rakayle Hier is an author and dreamer. She has enjoyed writing poems and stories for many years; mystery is one of her favorite to explore. If she isn't writing, you might find her riding her red roan horse into the Montana sunset, or sewing historical outfits. She has found a new way to share her passions at her blog "A Story Detective." She is inspired by writers and wants to inspire others to write.

Love's Mysterious Faith

Love is to feel the pain of another
as if it were your own.
To me love's beauty and miracle is when
like souls unite to mend and make.
Saw you from afar to see the you that you are.
Perhaps mystery is love
and love is mystery.
You with your two smiles
one to say I'm okay, one to say thank you.
A toast to the things we think.
Love is but the way you stand, sit and walk
that floods my eyes with the simple beauty of the you, you are.
You stand strong and fearless, though you hurt too.
Seldom could words echo off my lips, left speechless
out of respect I'm sure.
The mystery of love is that while human
you get to meet and love someone like yourself
and that is beautiful.

Jennifer Uncles

About the Author

One of my favorite adventures has been getting to be an aunt. You get the joy of loving and spoiling them. Enjoy gardening, reading books, the good classics ones we all hear of. Good wit and humor have always been a hereditary trait I've been blessed with. Also enjoy experiencing different cuisines and foods as well as coffee, espresso's and all they entail.

What Does 27 Look Like?

Hannah, what does twenty-seven
look like in Heaven?
Are there are bulletin boards to create?
Loaves of friendship bread to bake?

More lesson plans to think about?
Dancing and singing I have no doubt!
Here on earth I watch the snow fall,
thinking, I'll just give you a call,

to wish a Happy Birthday to you
and ask for a description of your new view.
But alas, no song from my head,
sending love from my heart instead.

Softly you whisper "I've found the key,
now all is well with me."
This is what a Mother wants to hear
even if the one she loves is not near.

God's loving arms still wrapped around her,
mystery solved, much needed gentle reminder.

Diane Johnson Cottrell

About the Author

Diane Johnson Cottrell lives in Hamilton MT with her husband Alton and their dog Samuel James. Diane writes a poem every year in memory of her daughter Hannah's birthday. This poem is from November 6, 2017.

A Simple Life (A Sonnet)

My God, you created a place for me
Surrounded by black holes and nothingness.
No reason life should spring from unlife be,
Yet here I am: multicellular, blessed.
Capable of creating life my own!
Two parts become one and life starts again.
Growing inside me a treasure unknown,
All the hairs counted and steps predestined.
All the joys in my life, rich history,
Beautiful mountains, sky everchanging.
The words to thank and praise a mystery;
You know already that and everything.
No good in me except for what You gave:
I was evil, dead. Why did Your blood save?

Courtney Duke Graves

About the Author

Courtney Duke Graves is a journalist working in Choteau, MT and a writer of all forms. When she's not playing with words, she enjoys exploring the Rocky Mountains with her husband, Cason, and their dog, Ghost.

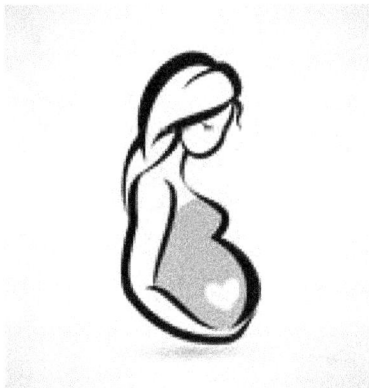

The Muse

magical spirit
source of inspiration
like a soft cloud
a puff of smoke gone in a moment
swept away by the changing winds
mystery beyond description
now she is gone
emptiness cries out like an addiction
or an intolerable fear
then submission
for I am again lost
more than ever before

James Van Ness

About the Author

Former corporate gypsy - BSChE University of North Dakota, MBA University of Connecticut, poet, hiker, skier and a lover of great independent film.

Nature's Bounty

Where is the mystery in a blade of grass and how it grows?
it's green one day and brown so soon, much like us:
We grow, flourish, and fade away all too quickly
Or so it seems. A babbling brook poses a mystery, too—
Flowing, rushing, and then reducing to a trickle
When droughts and flood challenge the landscape, altering it irrevocably.
How can we time our lives around the flourishing, fast-running brook
And the emerald green grass, when it's all so transient?
Maybe our task is not to worry
Because we'll never unravel the wonders posed by nature,
Our Maker's loving gift to provide us sustenance and succor,
To help us navigate the good times, and the bad.
Maybe we need to slow down, dream more
And worry less about our own insignificance
In the great, grand scheme of things.
Some will say, "Meditation is the Answer and the Key to Well-being."
I say, "Give me a good book, a hammock, a glass of iced tea
and Mozart tunes playing on the radio and I'm a happy camper,"
No longer confused. I'm still in awe
of Mother Nature's stunning mysteries.

Linda Granzow

About the Author

I enjoy writing poetry and have been doing so since I was in elementary school. This poem, as with many of my compositions, is in free verse. I find the latter to be non-inhibiting and I enjoy just letting my pen and mind go for it! My background is in liberal arts, the humanities, business/contract management, and education. Most of my career was spent as an educator, and although I'm now retired, I still consider myself to be a teacher with a creative streak.

Mystery?

The mystery unravels every day
With the rising and the setting of the sun.
Who faithfully sends it on its way?

The newborn pronghorn fawn can run
So quickly after being born in spring.
Who holds classes for this little one?

The seasons, with each passing month, do bring
Changes – to climate, plants, daylight, even sod.
Who redecorates the land and everything?

Life passes and we scarce do think it odd
That all is ordered on this earth we've trod.
Who directs, creates, adorns our world, but God.

Al Leland

About the Author

Mr. Leland graduated from Tabor College in Hillsboro, KS. before returning to Montana to teach. He taught all 30+ years in Big Sky Country and, for the past 17 years, has taught English here at his alma mater. In his years at LCHS, he taught creative writing, basic English, PE, as well as coached basketball and track. He spent 10 years serving as supervising teacher, and the last couple in the guidance department. He enjoys spending time in God's creation through camping, hunting, and fishing. He also loves spending time with family, especially his wife Connie and son Tom.

The Path

a large boulder blocks my path
just sitting there doing nothing
intrigued I can feel it's vibration
when I get close it becomes quiet
the stone turns cold if I try to touch it
I have tried reason
there is no response
something tells me to sit here and wait
meditate and pray for God's grace
I could walk around
continue on my path
but then I would miss the stubborn rock's
metamorphosis into a butterfly

James Van Ness

About the Author

Former Corporate Gypsy - BSChE University of North Dakota, MBA University of Connecticut, poet, hiker, skier and a lover of great independent film.

The Martial Artist

Hands of stone molded and folded.
Holds his own as he bows against defeat.

A tumble
a rumble
quite humble.

Ears are bleeding and broken
words seldom spoken.

Mystery in his eyes
tells no lies.

Dances on his feet
so neat
can't be beat.

Hairs in a tuffle
shirts a ruffle.

Sports a shiner well
it sure does swell.

For love of the game
what's his name?

Red badge of courage.

Jennifer Uncles

About the Author

My name is Jennifer. Born and raised in Montana. Montana because you get to experience the joy of every season. Enjoy baking as well as making jam. Poetry and writing inspire me because it takes you places, plus it is fun to rhyme and see what you can create. Writing takes the mind places, the same way art does, but in a different form. Writing does change and touch with its flow and depth.

Becoming One

They stand in silence suspended in time
thinking of the years that have tip-toed by

happy years
fragrant with the scent of love in bloom
charged with emotions running high

growing years
the mystery of two separate hearts
beating in perfect rhythm, secretly uniting as one

creation years
planting, sewing and waiting birth
love's full expression, two daughters and a son.

Was it that long ago when the sun burned hot
blinding the adversity of life, the toil
all the strength and binding

and now the sunset years when love
tried by fire casts it's golden glow
touched by the hand of God

Hand in hand through life
and now standing at eternity's door
the promise of love in completion, together forever more.

Susan Rayson

About the Author
Just a woman who enjoys putting words together when inspired.

Mystery

Ancient history
Discovered
Uncovered
Brought to light
Was outta sight
Found by luck
Gold was struck
Memory strained
Knowledge gained
Blessing remains

Christine Wichman

About the Author

I grew up in a small town called Hilger, Montana on a farm/ranch. In 7th grade Science class we had an assignment to write a poem. I wrote about birds. That seemed to spark my love of poetry, and I began reading poetry and writing my own as well. I am married and have no children. In my free time I enjoy helping out with Relay for Life, and various church activities. I hope to one day get a full book of poems published.

Churchill Said It First

"A Riddle Wrapped in a Mystery Inside an Enigma"...
what a beautiful way to sum up the game we play at times,
when given enough leeway to lead others astray.
Why do we engage in such subterfuge, with no hint of civility?
Do we think our time here is infinite?
Can we just succumb to insatiable needs?
Oh, but our needs are too often really wants,
When we ourselves are found wanting--and needing.
I wondered a lot why Winston Churchill coined his phrase
To describe the supposed response of a foe nation.
Perhaps he was attempting to console his countrymen,
Reassure them in the face of great, ominous odds
As statesmen are wont to do. Or maybe he was channeling
Some inner thoughts, fighting his own demons,
Trying to ease a battle of wills, right wrongs,
assuage his conflicted conscience
To help not only others, but also to support his aims.
Vagaries of human nature remain,
And the mysteries abide...
can we learn enough fast enough to save us from ourselves?

Linda Granzow

About the Author

I enjoy writing poetry and have done so since my grade school days. I tend to compose much of my work as free verse without the constraint of formal rules, mainly because I believe that, done well, it can still be very effective. My background is in liberal arts, the humanities, and business/contract management. A large part of my career was spent in education, and although I am now retired, I still think of myself as primarily an educator with a creative bent.

The Mystery of Time

The seed of time is flawless as it falls to the earth.
Amidst the apple blossoms
the humming of bees flying from tree to tree.
Let it be Adam said to Eve
you're the apple of my eye.

The coal pressed diamonds are the keys to young girl's heart
as he bleeds and pleads on bended knee, why me?

The bread of life etched in stone
dust to dust, ashes to ashes
I'll have a slice of life.
Who's to pay the price?

Water mixed with wine
the well spring of time pressed from grapes.
Fermenting yeast and grapes create a feast.
Eat of my flesh, drink of my blood.

Through the hourglass of time sifted by hand
I give you my hand to pass safely through this land.

Jennifer Uncles

About the Author

I'm the youngest sibling, having two older brothers. I enjoy fishing,
suppose it's the excitement, suspense of waiting and catching a fish.
Love the rush when you get a bite from a fish. My parents and I
share a anniversary and birthday together. Lucky them; I was born
on their anniversary, always been a special moment for us.

Little Man

History is mystery unveiled.
We are created to seek as much as to breath.
Some seek the tangible
hoping to satisfy the intangible thirst
to know the unfathomable God
who is mystery.
From Moses to Columbus
to all of us
we can't see beyond the horizon.
We chartered the seas
surveyed the entire earth.
Little man, look up to sky's if you can.
The mystery continues.
We've come to know mysteries
meant to be sought.
We trust in the promises
of the unfathomable eternal.

Jim Uncles

About the Author

Native Montanan born in Butte, Montana. Raised in Helena, raised my family in Belgrade for 36 years.

Deep Winter

It's -42 below outside this morning.
The sun ventures a cool yellow peek over the mountain's crest.
A pink glow still emanates from last night's yard light onto the
snowmound below it,
but even that is chill.
White smoke curls from every chimney with a certain downdraft.
It's cold.
And the mountain shrouds herself in white.
Still. Waiting. Wanting.
No companionship of skiers will color her lifts today;
no carefree soul to break her powder;
no daring traveler to challenge her couloirs this morning!
Even squirrels are quiet; curled tightly in their nests.
Bears sleep it off in thick fur coats, buried somewhere deep inside
surrounding hills.
Winter is here.
Its misty Wonderland beckons just outside my iced-up window...
Coat and boots taunt me.
But t's -42 below outside.
And the mountain shrouds herself in white...

Kristin Downer

About the Author

Kristin Downer is an over-fifty, native
"Montana Girl," avid Christ-Follower,
and mother of thirteen grown-kids,
blessings every one! Whether "painting
pictures" with words, watercolors, or
music notes, creating is definitely
Kristin's "happy place!"

Calling them in from the sun

The river rising,
an orange dog runs through the makeshift marsh after a young mallard –
I enter my body of wild chives and white lilacs,
taste buds purified drums blown blue with flax, sweet grass,
forgiveness that's not accusatory,
her echo heavy in an upturned palm.
The creek could be road,
daughter heron in a gold velvet hat,
son sage grouse, fast and close to earth.
Husband, not bird at all but something like the trees, the surety of seasons.
Do you have your compass?
Do you wear it locked around your neck?
The monsters have settled and I held Lyra, not yet two days.
There is nothing and everything under the bed.
I can't keep up with wildflowers.
We buried his placenta beneath the cherry tree eight years ago,
defrosted poppy in a metal bowl, guarded muscle in my hands.
All I want is this branch of starlight, bloom girl in red chair, head still,
held in Aspen's silent shudder – they grow into families.
Out of mist she rises, the way wood smoke rises, then disappears.

Gillian Kessler

About the Author

Gillian Kessler can be found dancing to loud music, teaching exuberant children to appreciate language at the Missoula International School, writing in the early morning when everyone is asleep and exploring the wilds of Montana with her beautiful family. She is replete with gratitude for the natural world.

Mysterious Chicken Thief

I lived just down the road from a friend of mine
He was a rancher and also a wilderness guide
A better friend would be awfully hard to find
A guy that any trail with whom you would ride

He had a guiding trip coming up that I was aware of
And would be gone for at least a couple of weeks
He had some chickens that he wanted me to take care of
There were only 20 of them that he usually keeps

I said "That's no problem, I'm around most of the time"
That would be easy, how hard could that possibly be
I had to let them out every morning, and that was fine
Feed and water them, this was easy as far as I could see

Then I locked them up at night so that they could roost
But, every morning there were fewer when I would count
Someone was stealing chickens, I knew they weren't loose
I had to try and catch them, so a camera I decided to mount

I found out my bandit wore a black mask over his eyes
I was down to one chicken, I had to do something soon
When I checked my camera, it was to my great surprise
My mysterious chicken thief had been a fat, old raccoon

Ron Peevey

About the Author

I have been writing poetry since I was 10 years old. I'm a retired General Contractor. I spent my last 10 years teaching high school kids how to build a house in Lewistown, MT. I have written 3 children's books and 1 western novel. I have a cowboy poetry book published called Buffalo Chips. I participate in the Lewistown Cowboy Poetry Gathering most years.

ILLIMITABLE

She carries and senses it.

Dreams, stained in Red.
Fears of loss.
A bond so much deeper than love.

She holds the hand
protects it with thorns.
Defends her blood beyond life.
Unconditional and everlasting.
The light is her anchor.
The darkness her run.
Temptations along the path,
but they fade
in the glow of the original.
She escapes from this unsearchable place.
With no fear.
She is the rock.

Julia Lawrance

About the Author

A European Patchwork-Mother of three little boys and wife of a Eastern-Montanan. In my mother-tongue - German - I loved the variety of expressions - spoken and written. Now I am trying out the American way. Professional for Office, University for industrial engineering, technical economy and marketing.

A Bitter Root

Walking towards the mist rising in cold early light,
My breath mingles with the autumnal spectral
Floating quietly above the mutable river.
Styx-like, it divides here from there,
Past from present.
Waters from the sky,
The earth, my eyes
Coalesce into a stream
That bears us all away.
A watery mystagogue
And catechism for my heart,
(Where a bitter root divides it as well),
It beckons the mysterious watersheds in my soul
To join its merciless current.
Misty phantoms of memory
Blur the farther shore.
A bitterrroot flower relieves pain.
Will this bitterroot mist relieve mine?

Valerie E. Hess

About the Author

Valerie E. Hess is a published author of both non-fiction and poetry as well as a professional church musician. A new resident of Montana, she also loves playing Mah Jongg and walking along the Bitterroot River.

A Clear Path

Life's a mystery...
We struggle and fall sometimes.
We can't find our way.
But dark becomes light
When we ask the right questions
And seek others' help.
Our paths may be strewn
With rocks and boulders galore!
God will set us straight.
Mo matter how long
Or how winding our road is
Light shines at the end.
It's like a spring day
With quick, new growth springing up;
We land on our feet.
No mystery here—
Our destiny lies ahead.
We should not look back.
My eyes have seen much, and I no longer question
Which path I must take.

Linda Granzow

About the Author

I enjoy writing poetry and have done so since a young elementary school age. The haiku form is one of my mainstays; I wrote this poem in seven haiku sections, with lines 19 and 20 comprising the last "stanza." My background is in liberal arts, the humanities, business/contract management, and education. I am now retired, but still think of myself as primarily an educator with a creative bent to my nature.

Who Can Explain?

Who can explain
Which at times seems so plain
The wetness of rain,
The absence of pain,
The flowers from seed,
Fruit from the trees,
The work of the bees,
And from where comes a sneeze?
Look at the night sky
As you gaze wonder why?
The stars tell a story
Of wondrous glory.
How can all this be?
Of all we endeavor
To explain to each other...
Tis' a mystery of
Love made plain.

Rose Koffler

About the Author

I am a reading enthusiast who dabbles in the writing of poetry.

Poems by Teens

A Dream?

I peered through the mist
wishing to see the secrets I know the forest keeps
slowly I wander
guided by a strong pull I feel inside
the pull is too strong to ignore
its grasp becomes tighter I begin to panic
the forest begins to whisper a sweet song to me
lulling me with its sweet words of safety and peace
suddenly a river is rushing and roaring at my feet
calling and crying, wishing for my company
everything vanishes except for the cries of the river, like a child
longing for its mother
I jump unable to resist the cries any longer
the river is cold, dark, and heartless like the blackest night
my head suddenly clears
what have I done
it is too late
the river has its cold grasp on me and there is nothing I can do
I let go...

Sophia Setters

About the Author

I am a tenth grader at Hellgate high school, who has a fascination for any kind of mystery. I love the outdoors and I love reading.

Glimpses

Glimpses are all I get

Every now and then you appear

Smiling as the light returns to your eyes

For a bit you're you again

But as the day goes on

The light fades

You become a stranger again

Tana Campbell

About the Author

My name is Tana Campbell, and I am a junior at Beaverhead County High School in Dillon, MT.

behind the gate

The ethereal scent flutters about

Waiting, wanting to be discovered

The iron door opens, creaking

Everything rushes out

A scream arises

Then there is nothing left

Outside the door the wind blows

Fluttering across the drying grass

It was let out, it was let out

No, that is impossible, a lie

But it was not false, it's possible

Definitely possible, right friend?

Kailani Myers

Sunbeams

Staring, the earth comes to a pause
Finishing our steps with a bang
Shattered glass
broken hearts
We lay afraid of the future living for the past
Swimming through blue stones
I slip down the page
the crisp lined paper folding half by half
line by line
She falls
swift as the needle that pricks three times
one, to the boy who fleetingly falls asleep
two, to the fabric that winds us apart
And three, to the old women with the wrinkled hands and the soft face
The ocean runs up her toes and down her fingers
She cries to the whales that keep her sound
With the diaphragm of an eagle
She soars through the city streets and the desert floors
Calmly the earth has stopped once again.

Mia Jakob

About the Author

Hi I'm a 13 year old writer. I enjoy skiing, hanging with friends and family and cooking. I wrote this poem because I have been having some rough past years. I had chronic ankle pain and, after 3 years of horrible days of pain, I got ankle surgery. Now I have had some time recovering and have had so much extra time to think about the past. This is one of my poems that I wrote about my deep feelings. Thanks for your time.

Whisper of the Shadows

Her steps are deathly silent.
Nothing in the forest breaths,
only the shadows hear the whispers of death as she passes.
A fool is singing nearby.
She freezes, smiling wickedly.
She smells the victory in the air,
tastes it on her lips.
She sees the fool.
She begins to climb up a tree.
He sits alone, by a fire oblivious to what looms above.
She waits for the right moment.
Now.
She leaps.
The fool barely screams, for death claims him,
Without mercy.

Rudi Evans

About the Author

I live near Missoula, Montana and love writing stories/poems. I am 14 years old and have grown up with stories and animals. I have always loved reading and it inspires a lot of stories I think up. This poem was something that can be interpreted as anything in anyone's mind. As long you can imagine it, it can become real. Trust me. When I was younger, I thought that I had magic (it might be!). Now that I am older, I know that it is, but it shows itself in the strangest ways! So never stop believing, no matter what! I hope that everyone will get to read more of my creations!

Secrets Untold

What secrets do those eyes hold?
Dark, dusty caves growing old
I know you've had your share of heartache
But what can you handle until your heart will fully break?

I observe the contours of your face, your deep hollow cheeks
Inside your mouth untold secrets reek
I know you need to speak, you need to tell
Your wonders, worries, anxiety putting you under a spell

Pictures are worth a thousand words, but looks are ten-thousand
I know the hurting, deep down you are drowning
I need you to speak to me, instead you glance
Your eyes pound with fear, give me a chance

I should've known you were going to leave
You went home with a gun up your sleeve
You wanted to talk, but instead your mouth closed
Your life was already gone, your heart enclosed

I guess I should've figured your mystery, while I had the chance
I like to think in Heaven you can dance
You're free, happy, any sorrows are gone
But you've left me unanswered, I went wrong

Paris Becker

About the Author
Paris Becker is a student at Fairfield High
School in Montana. In her spare time, she
reads, sings at her church, Fresh Life, and
attempts to golf regardless of her score. She is
surrounded by 4 loving siblings, three dogs,
two cats, four ducks, 15 chickens, and two
amazing parents. She hopes to be an English
teacher after high school and college.

Pain

Darkness.
Pitch black.
Emptiness.
Scratchy fabric pressed to my eyes.
Cold stone digging into shoulder blades.
Metal bands constricting wrists and ankles.
Heart ramming against ribs, mice squeaking.
Door screeching open, heavy hitched steps.
Shallow, rotten breath on my face.
Chair scraping across floor too loudly.
Stinging hot line spreading from wrist to forearm,
Warm blood sliding down my flesh.
Loud scream filling ears.
Blood pounding in head, thud-thud-thud.
Another searing line sinking into ankle flesh.
Knife blade biting into my skin.
Agony erupting behind my eyes.
Darkness.
Pitch black.
Emptiness.

Savannah Deuter

About the Author

My name is Savannah Deuter and I am in eighth grade. I live in Missoula with my parents and awesome little sis.

The Wonder of Fall

Leaves metamorphosize from emeralds
into gorgeous gold and rubied hues,
Pumpkins, squash, corn and zucchinis ripen into sumptuous jewels,
Geese glide into formation as they honk their goodbyes,
mysteriously knowing their destination,
Determined bucks fight ferociously for the right of beloved female,
Skies turn from vibrant blue to a dull, cloudy gray,
Bringing the dread of winter that shifts into the hope of spring,
A mystery of the Maker.

Emmy Fanguy

About the Author

Hi, my name is Emmy and I am 13. I love nature (a lot!) and wrote this poem at a meadow by my house. I am the oldest of five kids and have two pets: a guinea pig named Yomi and a dog named Sweet Pea. I hope you enjoy reading my poem!

Fear

Have you ever experienced fear?
True fear that seems to never go away?
That one feeling that follows you everywhere
That constant nightmare that's determined to stay
That deep feeling you get deep in your gut
The sweat that drips off your palms
The panic rises and your breathing picks up
The loud beating your heart expresses as if it's a bomb
Your neck hair will slowly stand up
You'll wonder if it'll ever go away
But you realize it's forever by your side
It'll follow you day by day
True fear is something that haunts you
Like the boogey man hiding under your bed as you try to sleep
Waiting for you to drift off so it can attack
Fear is a feeling that's just too deep.
Fear is powerful but you are stronger
Don't wonder how you can live with this nightmare
Learn to look fear right in the eyes
Learn to say "I accept this dare"

Faith Stenger

About the Author

Hi, I'm Faith and I was 17 at the time this poem was written and submitted. Writing has always been a hobby of mine. I write constantly in my daily life. I write poems, stories, songs and even little quotes.

Malady

For years I do not reveal

Until the time is unfortunate

You feel ill as I appear

Feel my chill in your bones

My presence is known

Your family knows of me

You all fear my presence

Plead for me to leave

But if I leave, so do you

Tana Campbell

About the Author

My name is Tana Campbell, and I am a junior at Beaverhead County High School in Dillon, MT.

The Place

A dark dreary room with no windows
where no one is and no one knows
how far away it goes and lives.
It lives in the dark and light
for it has no sight for that it knows.
Who is the place
where is the place
no one knows such a face.
It's a beat up cabin
with a snow covered roof
in the Rocky Mountains.
Who knows what the place is
or who the place is
but we believe in the place
because when we're in that place we're sad and angry
but when we're in another place we're happy and full of joy
for that is the place no one knows
and no one cares for
that is the place.

Natalyn Meyer

About the Author

I'm a 16 year old who finds joy in writing and cooking. When you're happy or when you're sad, you are in a place where only you know where you go; it's a void; a ray of sunshine; it's a mystery where we are, but nonetheless, it's a place that we go.

Your Identity

Clueless am I until I see all the clues
You've given to me of Your identity
The ocean, depth unknown
The thunder that rolls across this rugged prairie of cowboy pride.
These strange dark skies that give into the bright sunrise
Painting the canvas some golden dyes.
The Mystery of the ocean
Stretches out your love.
The mystery of the thunder
Booms you the mighty one.
The mystery of the sun that never fails
To rise above these rugged hills.
The Mystery isn't so hard now that I see
Everything you've given to me of Your identity.
My Father, My Creator, My King the answers
You give are hidden in everything.

Amariah Hier

About the Author

Amariah is a Montana cowgirl who loves riding her horse, reading and writing stories, studying Bible, roping, ice skating, and playing her fiddle. She dreams of someday flying an airplane and finishing her green broke. Meanwhile, she's helping with the ranch and playing air-soft with her brothers.

Publisher's Prerogative

Through the Glass
(a Shakespearean sonnet)

Its shimmer and its promise draw me near.

A spark within prompts me toward what I see.

I find the eyes of one I love and fear;

She's gazing out of my eyes back at me.

How long I stood there I cannot recall

To contemplate what beauty I might find

And search out every blemish, every flaw

To bind them each securely in my mind.

But had I chanced to look beyond my face

I would have gazed into another's eyes,

For there He stood with patience and with grace

To teach me how to see through all the lies.

Forever He will beckon and will bade.

To see Him I must search and I must fade.

S. E. Thomas

He must become greater;
I must become less.
John 3:30

For now we see in a mirror, dimly, but then we will see face to face.
Now I know only in part; then I will know fully,
even as I have been fully known.

I Corinthians 13:12

About This Collection

The poems in this book were collected through an annual state-wide call for writers of all ages. It opens September 1st and runs through October 15th. It is FREE to submit—which makes it perfect for individuals and for use as a class project for students of any age.

If you are interested in submitting a piece to this collection or sharing this information with a teacher, a friend, or a family member, please bookmark the following informational resources:

Website: www.TheDramaticPen.com

Facebook: www.facebook.com/TheDramaticPen

Twitter: @TDPPress

Please sign up for our free, monthly e-newsletter through the home page on our website. All upcoming contests, calls for writers, and new products are announced there, as well as tips for writers, a book of the month, a tried and true recipe, and more! We hate junk mail as much as you do, so we promise not to fill up your inbox, and you can unsubscribe at any time.

About the Editor

S. E. Thomas, M.A.

is a multi-published, award-winning author, editor, and publisher. A wife, mother, and avid comedian and story-teller, she lives and works in Lolo, Montana. She has her master's degree in philosophy and is working on a seminary certificate. She writes biblical historical fiction, inspirational fiction, YA dystopia, drama, and Christian non-fiction. She works at the local Care Net Pregnancy Resource Center. Susan is married to Dr. Aaron Thomas, and they have three children: Yesenia, Dakota, and Novik.

Please follow her author's page on Amazon and connect with her via Facebook and Twitter at:

www.facebook.com/AuthorSEThomas

@susanethomas1

More From:

@TDPPress
www.thedramaticpen.com
facebook.com/thedramaticpen

Into the Beautiful
Poetry by Montana Artists Series

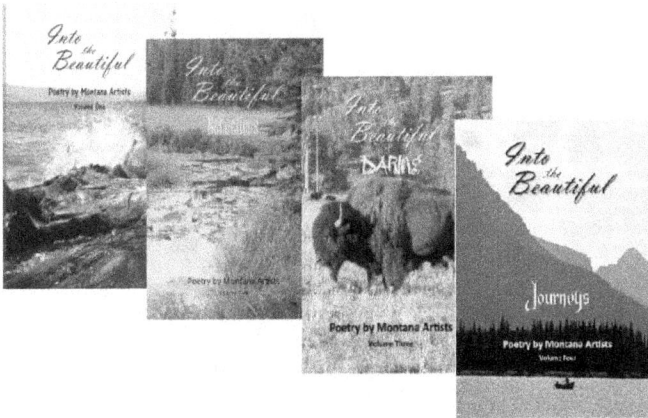

"Into the Beautiful: Poetry by Montana Artists" is a series of poetry books by Montana artists of all ages. These works of art and creativity were collected from Montana artists of all ages. To find out more, please visit our website at www.TheDramaticPen.com.

Longing for Rest
A Novella
S. E. Thomas

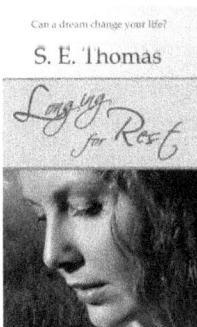

One heartbroken woman battles insomnia. Another cannot escape the coma trapping her between dreams and reality. Though they have never met, through a miraculous crossing of consciousness, they find themselves together on a grassy hill surrounded by a mysterious fog. In this dream world, Amy and Gracie form an unusual friendship. But will fear, pain, and betrayal follow them and spoil this haven? Will they finally be able to rest? Can a dream change your life? Available in paperback ($7.99) or eBook ($2.99 from Kindle or Nook.)

The Scrolls of the Nevi'im Series:

Book I: Habakkuk's Plea: A Prophet of Elohim
Book II: Habakkuk's Plea: Evil Persists
Book III: Habakkuk's Plea: Elohim Answers
S. E. Thomas

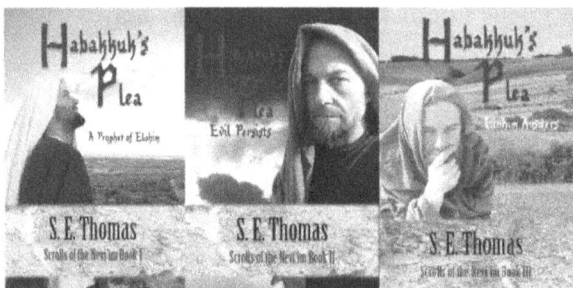

The Sixth Hour
Book I of the Holy Land Mysteries Series
S. E. Thomas

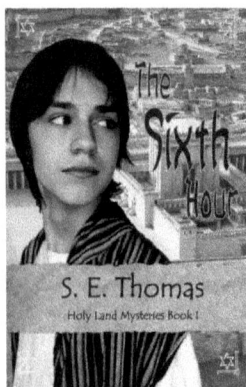

Can Darash, a Jewish teenager, track a killer, rescue his family from ruin, and discover the truth about Yeshua? The rebel, Yeshua, drove the merchants and moneychangers from the Temple with a whip. Hours later, one of them was murdered. Now fifteen-year-old Darash must find a way to protect his family from poverty even as he struggles with the grief of losing his father. When another murder is committed, Darash finds himself searching for a dangerous killer and relying on an old, blind basket-weaver for help. But will he be able to expose the killer before the killer finds him?

The Holy Land Mysteries Series
Darash's adventure continues with…

Book II: The Brazen Altar

Force Down the Night
Age of Technics Trilogy, Book I
S. E. Thomas

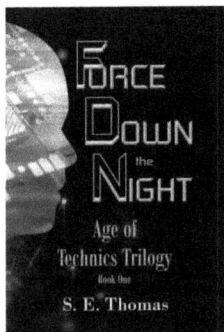

Galaxy, a skinny fifteen-year-old girl with long white hair, doesn't know why Absalom spoils her so much. Especially since she's just an undersized CC—a member of the Commodity Class—a class of expendable slaves. Absalom owns Absalom Industries, including AI Tower, the most iconic structure of post-apocalyptic Washington D.C. As a mass producer of CCs, Absalom can have any personal CC he wants—a super smart Wit, a powerful Warrior, or even a sexy Pristine. Instead he chose Galaxy, one of the Naturals—a sickly, petite girl who prefers to nap in the sun instead of attend class. When Galaxy discovers that Absalom is dying, she realizes her days of privilege are at an end. A new executive order will cut the CC population down by a third. Galaxy and her best friend, Needle, will be among those sent to the incineration chamber. Now Galaxy has a choice to make. Use what's left of her privilege to secure safety for herself and Needle... or join the doomed CC rebellion.

A Reason To Celebrate
A Full-Length Christmas Production
S. E. Thomas

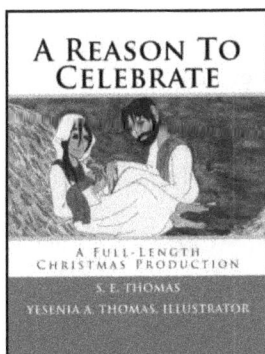

For most, Christmas is a time filled with joy. But for many, Christmas can be a difficult season. But let us consider a moment what Scripture tells us of the first Christmas. What really happened? For the first time, God Himself —the Creator of the Universe, the King of Kings, the Everlasting Father—stepped into our world! He stepped in— not to enjoy the wealth or the beauty or the joys— but to experience our suffering, our longings, and our sorrows. From the moment of His birth, He experienced far from ideal circumstances. Yet, we remember His words, "In this world you will have trouble. But take heart! I have overcome the world."

Interactive Mystery Party Games
for Teens and Adults
S. E. Thomas

Who Invited the Stiff to Dinner?
Murder at Surly Gates
Accuracy
Let Them Eat Cake

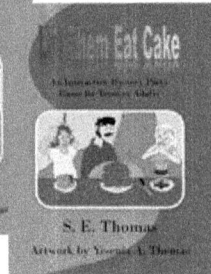

Acting Out Loud
Christian Skits for All Occasions
S. E. Thomas

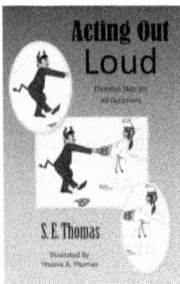

Whether you are a pastor looking for a skit to help drive home your message, a ministry leader desiring a dramatic reading to speak God's love at a retreat or conference, or a youth group leader hoping to spice up a youth meeting, we have the material you're looking for! Find over thirty skits, short plays, and dramatic readings that cover the following areas: Biblical Tales, Christian Living, Evangelism, Special Events, Holidays.

Lazy Dog
carol fields brown

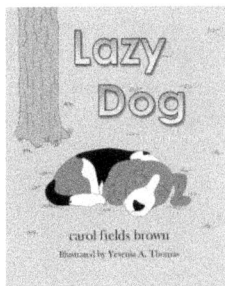

"The quick brown fox jumps over the lazy dog." This sentence is called a pangram. A pangram contains every letter of the English alphabet at least one time. This storybook starts with this famous pangram. The Lazy Dog and the Fox start us on an animal adventure. You can write the sentences and color the pictures. At the end of the book is a chart to help you make up your own sentences. At first you may need help, but soon you will be able to make your own. Every sentence can become a story. Do you know why the Fox jumped over the lazy dog? I wonder…. What do you think? This coloring book provides an opportunity for young learners to explore the intricacies of the English language, practice their handwriting, and explore a variety of animal behaviors in a fun and creative way. Full-color illustrations, matching coloring pages, and lines for handwriting practice are also included.

Is My Faith My Own?
A Resource for Christian Young People
Leaving Home for the First Time
S. E. Thomas

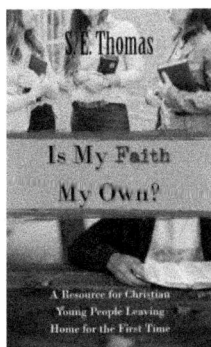

Everything was going along fine... then you got out on your own and realized it's your responsibility to get the rest of your life right. From here on out, if you're going to follow God, you're going to be doing it on your own. You can no longer coast by on your parents' faith, your pastor's understanding, or your youth leader's morals. Now it's up to you. And you have some questions: Is my faith real? Is it growing? Is it my own? (A *Finding Hope Resource Guide*.)

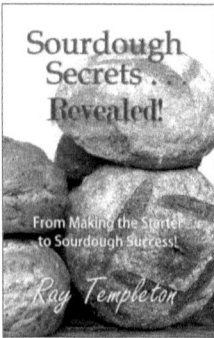

Sourdough Secrets… Revealed!
From Making the Starter to Sourdough Success!
Ray Templeton

Step-by-step instructions that will allow you to make your own starter, make your first loaf, and even learn to make sourdough bread in your bread machine.

Complex Simplicity:
How Psychology Suggests Atheists are Wrong about Christianity
Dr. Lucian Gideon Conway III

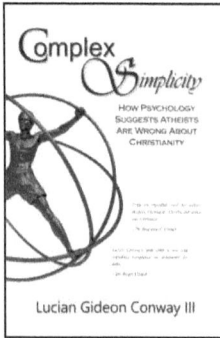

In *Complex Simplicity*, prominent psychology researcher Dr. Lucian Gideon Conway III addresses the modern atheist attack on the psychological effectiveness of the Christian religion. As an expert in the science of cognitive complexity, Dr. Conway uses scientific research and personal narratives to argue that Christianity is an effective guide for reconciling the many complexities built into the human psyche. Directly contradicting what many modern atheists believe, he shows that, in approaching human psychology from a complex perspective, Christianity meets our complex needs with complex solutions. To Christian believers, he offers psychological reasons to believe their faith yields positive benefits. To skeptics, he offers a challenge to the growing cultural belief that Christianity is both simple-minded and ineffective. *Complex Simplicity* is important reading for anyone curious about the intersection of Christian teaching and human psychology.

Daily Life in Bible Times
Small Group Study
S. E. Thomas

Workbook & Leader Guide Editions

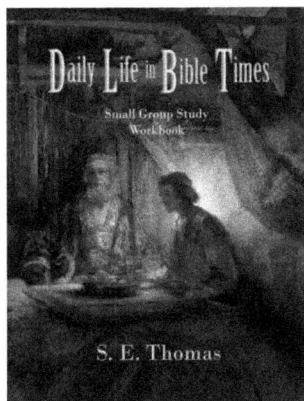

Come face to face with the people you read about in Scripture by exploring what their daily lives would have looked like. Learn how a young man selected and courted his bride, what occupations they had and how they trained for them, how infants were cared for, and how the ancients mourned and buried their dead. We will also look at the economic and political climate, learn about crime and punishment, and even find out what they ate and how they dressed. And as you come to know the culture of Jesus Christ, you will see Him more clearly, as well. *This is a 10-week Bible study.*

Please Visit Us Again!

Find books, study guides, plays, skits, mystery party games, fundraising resources, free downloadable program templates, writers' resources, and much more at:

www.TheDramaticPen.com

Write To Bless The World

www.ingramcontent.com/pod-product-compliance
Lightning Source LLC
Chambersburg PA
CBHW071742020426
42331CB00008B/2130